DISHES WITHOUT MEAT

OVEN TEMPERATURES

F	C	GAS	TYPE
150°	70°	Lowest	coid
175°	80°	Lowest	cold
200°	100°	Lowest +	cold +
225°	110°	$\frac{1}{4}$	very cool
250°	130°	$\frac{1}{2}$	
275°	140°	1	cool
300°	150°	2	
325°	170°	3	very moderate
350°	180°	4	moderate
375°	190°	5	moderate to
400°	200°	6	moderately hot
425°	220°	7	hot
450°	230°	8	
475°	240°	9	very hot
500°	250°	–	
525°	250°	–	
550°	290°	–	

METRIC CONVERSION

WEIGHT

1 Ounce   25 grams
2 Ounce   50 grams
3 Ounce   75 grams
4 Ounce   100 grams
5 Ounce   125 grams
6 Ounce   150 grams
7 Ounce   175 grams
8 Ounce   200 grams
$\frac{1}{2}$ Pound = 200-250 grams.

1 Pound = 500 grams.

VOLUME

$\frac{1}{8}$ Pint   60 Millilitre
$\frac{1}{4}$ Pint 125 Millilitre
$\frac{1}{2}$ Pint 250 Millilitre
$\frac{3}{4}$ Pint 375 Millilitre
1 Pint 500 Millilitre

1 ounce = 25 grams as advised by The Metrication Working Party of the United Kingdom Federation for Education in Home Economics.

DISHES
WITHOUT MEAT

by
AMBROSE HEATH

BARRIE & JENKINS
COMMUNICA-EUROPA

This edition published 1976
by Barrie and Jenkins Ltd
24 Highbury Crescent
London N5 1RX

Printed in Great Britain by
REDWOOD BURN LIMITED
Trowbridge and Esher

CONTENTS

FOREWORD

THIS is not a vegetarian cookery book, although foodstuffs generally associated with vegetarian diet often form the basis of the recipes given here. Meat stock may be used in some, bacon fat employed in the cooking or a garnish of ham, tongue or chicken's livers added to others, but as a matter of fact these ingredients can be easily adapted or varied so as to bring the recipes within the range of those who do not eat meat.

The book's main intention is to show that dishes of rice, macaroni, haricot beans and the like are by no means necessarily uninteresting. Ordinary savoury rice, plainly cooked haricot beans or macaroni cheese can become deadly dull through repetition, but here will be found many ways of serving their main ingredient which are unusual and attractive, not merely by their own intrinsic merit but by the charm of the various garnishes that will enhance their appearance and comprehensive flavour. A section on Potato dishes which can be served as a main course concludes the book.

The many famous dishes of France, Italy, Central Europe and the East offer entrancing examples of this versatility, and for whatever reason we do not wish to serve meat as the main course of the meal, here are substitutes to compare favourably with the more usual meat dishes by their novelty and deliciousness and will also, I confidently hope, help to lend new interest and variety to the table of the enterprising hostess.

A. H.

RICE

I HAVE begun with Rice because of all the dishes that follow those made with rice possess for me the greatest personal appeal. It is sad to think that for the great majority of people the charm of rice is known only in a milk pudding, as an accompaniment to curries and in the kedgeree which, like macaroni cheese, has become almost a national dish. How many other delicious manifestations it can assume will be discovered in the ensuing pages, and I can do no more than recommend my readers very highly to try and to enjoy them all.

There are many sorts of rice and, to be at their best, different dishes demand different types 'for their making. The sort for accompanying curries and for making the Indian Pillaus or pilaffs should be Patna rice, while the Italian risotto demands a fatter kind of grain, if I may use the term, as witness the large rosy-coloured variety from Piedmont that used to be obtainable here but now must be superseded by the Carolina type from the New World. The greatest success both gastronomically and dietetically will be obtained from unpolished rice when available, but the main thing is to endeavour to buy the best possible rice of its kind.

The recipes that follow will exemplify the many different uses to which this prince of grains can be put.

The simplest form of cooked rice, of course,

is that used as an accompaniment to curries, and strange as it may seem, there are still a great many people who simply cannot, or will not, cook it properly. This is how it should be done.

Rice for Curries

First wash the Patna rice in several cold waters. This is best done by putting the rice into a colander or sieve, plunging this into a bowl of cold water and rubbing the rice between the fingers so as to rid it of starchy particles, and renewing the water as required. It should then be soaked for at least twenty minutes in cold water. Now it is most important that the rice has plenty of room to cook in the water, so for a pound of rice you must use six pints of water, which you will have ready boiling in a large clean pan. Add the drained rice to the boiling water with a dessertspoonful of salt (this is important, for too many people cook their rice unsalted which robs it of much of its flavour), give it a stir with a wooden spoon to stop it from sticking in a lump at the bottom of the pan, and let it boil quickly for ten to twelve minutes. When it is soft enough for the grain to be crushed lightly between the finger and thumb, it is ready. Now pour the whole contents of the pan, water and all, into a colander, and pour rather less than half a teacupful of cold water over the grains to separate them. Drain thoroughly, and that is all.

There are so many variations of curry that it would be impossible even to indicate them all here, but as a vegetable or fish curry makes an admirable meatless dish, I give an excellent curry sauce, which although it may be a trifle unorthodox, in so far as it does not contain coconut milk, is to my mind very delicious, and certainly very useful on the score of its simplicity.

Curry Sauce

Fry two small sliced onions and a little bit of garlic a light brown (but on no account let them burn), then stir in half a tablespoonful of curry powder, or curry powder and paste mixed, salt to taste, and stir for a few minutes over the heat to let the curry powder mellow. Now add half a pound of quartered tomatoes and a tea-cupful of water, which should make a thick paste. Do not use any flour for thickening whatever you do, but if the sauce is not thick enough let it reduce over the heat until it is. This sauce can be used just as it is, with the tomato skins removed, or it can be rubbed through a sieve. Let it cook for a quarter of an hour or so, then add whatever is to be curried in it, put on the lid, and leave on a low heat for twenty minutes or so.

The sauce described above is suitable for heating up ready-cooked food, and a great many very pleasant curries can be made in this way, for example, of hard-boiled eggs, tinned shrimps, prawns or lobster, cooked cauliflower or potatoes or mixed vegetables, all of which can be prettily garnished with such extras as green peas or beans to give an additional touch of colour.

But one of the main delights of a curry are the little dishes of accompaniments: chutneys of several kinds, Bombay Ducks and Poppadums (which can be bought in tins), shredded or desiccated coconut and so on.

Pillau Rice

The best-known savoury rice from India is the *Pillau Rice*, and this is how it is made. Again use Patna rice, and a shallow saucepan or sauté-pan with a close-fitting lid. Fry a large onion and two cloves of garlic, both chopped, in half a pound of margarine until golden with twelve cloves, twelve whole cardamoms, two two-inch sticks of cinnamon and half a teaspoonful of whole allspice. Then add a pound of rice and fry on for four or five minutes on a low heat, tossing the rice lightly. Now add half a teaspoonful of saffron steeped in half a teacupful of warm water, and enough boiling water to cover the rice by an inch or two. Cover the pan tightly, and cook on a very low heat until the rice has absorbed all the water, and is perfectly cooked in separate grains. At the last stir in lightly four ounces of sultanas and two ounces of blanched sweet almonds first lightly fried in margarine.

This is the rice to accompany the well-known kebabs, which are mixtures of meat or fish or vegetables impaled on skewers and then generally grilled. Or, if preferred, cooked prawns, for example, or a macedoine of cooked vegetables can be incorporated with the pillau rice after it has been made.

Before we leave the rice dishes of India, here is a very simple one which has a great appeal to many.

Yellow Rice

First, using a deep pan with a close-fitting lid, fry a tablespoonful of chopped onion and a very little minced garlic with a single clove in two ounces of margarine for about five minutes until the onions are golden, then add half a teaspoonful of ground turmeric and half a saltspoonful of ground cummin seed. Stir and cook for another minute or two, then add half a pound of washed and soaked Patna rice, with salt to taste. Stir and cook five minutes longer, then add enough boiling water to cover the rice by an inch or so, cover tightly, and cook over a very low heat until the rice is done and the water all absorbed. Be careful not to stir the rice while it cooks, but just lift it up now and then with a fork or metal spoon so that it cooks evenly.

This is the orthodox recipe, but I have found myself that I enjoy rather more a savoury rice of this kind flavoured with the turmeric and half a bay leaf (whole not crushed) and with the cummin omitted.

As we come nearer West, the rice dishes become less spicy, and in Greece a favourite Pilaff is flavoured only with tomato.

Pilaff (Greece)

Put a tablespoonful of butter or margarine into a saucepan over a moderate heat, add the pulp of a tomato, a few tomato slices or a little tinned tomato purée and a dash of salt, and when it is all quite hot, add a breakfastcupful of rice and stir over the heat for a few minutes until the rice is coloured all over.   Then add two breakfastcupfuls of boiling water and a little more salt, and cook over a low heat, closely covered, until the rice is ready and the water absorbed. If preferred, this and other rice dishes of a similar nature can be cooked in a moderate oven instead of on top of the stove.

It is in Italy that we find the rice dish most suited to our European taste, the famous *Risotto*, which varies according to the district in which it is made. Unless otherwise directed, the white risotto is the basis for most of these dishes, and this is how it is cooked:

White Risotto

Put an ounce and three-quarters of butter in a saucepan and fry a small chopped onion in it until lightly browned.   Then add a pound of rice and mix well together so that the rice is coated with the fat. Then add a pint and a half of boiling white stock, and cook for fifteen minutes or so, covered, until the rice is done, and the stock absorbed. Season them with salt and pepper, and the rice is ready to be completed by adding another ounce and three-quarters of butter and three and a half ounces of grated Parmesan cheese.

It must be remembered that the flavour of the risotto depends entirely upon the flavour of the stock, which can be either veal, chicken or vegetable.

White Risotto (Milanese)

Here the pound of rice is first boiled in salted water for a quarter of an hour, then drained on a sieve and cold water poured over it. It is then heated and mixed with grated Parmesan cheese as above, and served with the following sauce poured over and mixed with it. Put three and a half ounces of butter in a saucepan and cook in it a chopped clove of garlic or two and a few sage leaves until the garlic is pale gold. Pour this all over the rice when the butter is foaming hot.

Risotto (Florence)

When the rice as for White Risotto is half-cooked, stir in some chopped and fried chicken's

livers. Finish cooking and stir in grated
Parmesan cheese as before. The livers can
be cooked in brown gravy first, if preferred.

Risotto with Dublin Bay Prawns

Make the risotto with fish stock made with
the shells and claws of some Dublin Bay Prawns,
seasoning with salt and pepper. When it is
ready, stir in lightly the tails of the prawns,
which have first been floured and fired in olive
oil.

Risotto with Vegetable Marrow

Add pieces of cooked and lightly fried vegetable marrow or pumpkin to a White Risotto.

Risotto Milanaise

This differs from the others in so far as wine
is used in the cooking. It is perhaps the most
delicious of all of them.

Fry without browning in two ounces of
butter a small chopped onion and two ounces
of finely chopped beef marrow. Then add a
pound of rice, and cook for ten minutes, stirring all the time with a wooden spoon. Now
add half a teaspoonful of saffron powder, three
tablespoonfuls of white wine, and gradually a
pint and a half of boiling beef or chicken stock,

and after mixing well together, season with salt and pepper. Cook the risotto in the usual way, and when it is ready, stir in another two ounces of butter and four ounces of grated Parmesan cheese. Serve as hot and as quickly as possible.

It is obvious that for ordinary enjoyment the exact ingredients of these *risotti* need not always be scrupulously adhered to, and cooks will soon find out for themselves the many delicious mixtures that they can invent or improvise. But these are the actual Italian recipes, and will show the way this very admirable dish can be produced.

And by the way if by any chance there should be any risotto left over, it can be treated like this:

Fried Risotto

Spread the rice thinly in a frying-pan in which you have first heated a little butter, and when it begins to brown lightly on one side, turn it over and fry the other until the finished object is a large golden fritter.

Kedgeree

This popular dish, usually made with rice and smoked haddock, has come to us through the Indian *Kitchri*, which is of a more elaborate nature. The great secret in making the English type is to use plenty of butter, or even margarine, though butter is to be preferred since it is the buttery flavour that makes the rice so delicious.

The rice is first boiled and dried in the same way as for *Rice for Curries* (page 10), and the butter is melted in a large pan. Into this is first put the pieces of fish, etc., that you want to use, so that they impart some of their flavour to it, and then the rice is added and carefully stirred in with a fork, so that it does not mash at all. In my opinion plenty of black pepper should also be added, but this is a matter of taste. Hard-boiled egg is also an essential, the roughly chopped whites being mixed in with the rice, and the yolks sieved coarsely and sprinkled on top with a chopping of parsley. This, like all rice dishes, must be served as hot as possible, and for those with a savoury palate there is no harm at all in mixing in a little grated cheese or handing some separately, though to my mind the plain dish is all that can be desired.

Those who have only eaten Kedgeree made with smoked haddock should try a few variations. Fresh cooked salmon is ineffable, and lobster, shrimps, prawns or even crab make extremely delicious dishes, and here again, except in the case of the salmon, cheese could be added.

A meaty Kedgeree can be made with roughly chopped ham or tongue in the same way, and even corned beef or other luncheon meats can be pressed into service here.

Jambalaya

What may perhaps be called a kind of Kedgeree is the *Jambalaya* of Creole cookery. In its simplest form it consists of the following:

Boil a breakfastcupful of rice in salted water for thirteen minutes, then drain and dry in the usual way. Now chop up a large onion and a clove of garlic, and fry them golden in some butter or margarine. Add half a pound of quartered tomatoes, and mash them with a wooden spoon to extract the juice. Now put the boiled rice in a deep pan with the onions and tomatoes and their juices, and add whatever you are going to use in the Jambalaya, small fried sausages or pieces of cooked or tinned crab, lobster, shrimps, or prawns. Mix all well together, season with salt, pepper, a dash of cayenne pepper and half a red chilli pepper, finely chopped, put on the lid, cover the pan and cook very gently over a low heat for thirty to forty minutes, stirring now and then.

When I was a schoolboy, I was fortunate in having an aunt who lived near enough to my school to enable me to spend my Sunday luncheon-times with her family. She was a Portuguese, and it was in her home that I first tasted the delights of a brown rice which I will call Portuguese Rice. Long after I had grown up, her daughter sent me this recipe:

Portuguese Brown Rice

Fry a large onion, chopped finely, in dripping or other suitable fat until *almost* burned, then pour in hot water, add a little salt, and boil until the water is quite brown and of a good oniony flavour. Strain off the onion, and cook the rice in the brown water, add a little more of the fat and a few crushed peppercorns, and serve very hot. This is rather vague, but I suggest that if you cook it in the same way as recommended for *Risotto*, that is to say in the oven and in the proportions of a cupful of rice to two cupfuls of the onion water, adding the fat at the end, you will achieve the same result. My cousin added that sausages or rissoles should be served on top of the rice and that it should be surrounded with cooked peas or sliced potatoes, but my recollection of this superlative dish is that it was generally used to accompany any kind of meat dish instead of potatoes.

Some other rice dishes that may be found useful are these:

Curried Rice

Mix lightly together with a fork three breakfastcupfuls of boiled and drained rice, a level teaspoonful of curry powder, three teaspoonfuls of anchovy paste, two beaten egg-yolks, and cayenne pepper to taste. Heat through to cook the egg slightly, and serve.

Curried Rice (2)

Brown half a pound of rice and two minced onions in an ounce of margarine or butter, add a tablespoonful of curry powder, and cook on for four or five minutes. Mix well together and pour in a pint and a half of boiling stock, season with salt, boil for ten minutes, then cover and simmer slowly for another forty minutes. Serve with fried onions and grilled tomatoes.

American Rice

Shred up the heart of a small cabbage finely. Put two tablespoonfuls of olive oil into a saucepan, add the cabbage and two breakfastcupfuls of rice, and stir for a few minutes over a low heat, so that the oil coats the other ingredients. Then add four breakfastcupfuls of water, two ounces of sultanas and a seasoning of salt and pepper, put on the lid and cook until the rice and cabbage are tender, which will take about half an hour.

Buttered Rice

Cook the rice in the usual way, drain it well and dry it. Now in a hot pan stir into it a little butter and a well-beaten egg, with a spoonful or two of chopped parsley or chives, and cook just long enough for the egg to set lightly. Stir with a fork before serving.

Golden Rice

Fry two chopped onions in two ounces of butter or margarine, add half a pound of rice and go on frying until the rice is golden-brown. Then add a pint and a half of boiling water, season with salt and pepper, and cook for about half an hour until the rice is tender. Serve sprinkled with grated cheese and melted butter which you have allowed to brown on top of the dish in a hot oven or under the grill. Fried or grilled mushrooms are good with this.

Rice à la Grecque

Cook half a pound of rice in a pint and a half of well-flavoured fish stock, then add a tablespoonful or so of diced salami sausage, a finely shredded lettuce, three tablespoonfuls of cooked or tinned green peas, and if you can manage it a tablespoonful of chopped sweet red pepper (pimiento).

Rice à la Portugaise

Brown half a pound of rice with a tablespoonful of chopped onions in two ounces of butter, and add half a pound of roughly chopped tomatoes, two sweet red peppers (pimientos) skinned and chopped, and a pint and a half of good stock, boiling. Cook for about half an hour after seasoning rather highly, and on serving sprinkle with a little melted butter.

Rice à la Turque

Put half a pound of rice and a chopped onion into a pint and a half of good fish stock, and cook for half an hour. Then season if necessary, add a pinch of saffron powder and a little butter or margarine and serve with stewed tomatoes or a tomato purée.

Rice and Cheese

Grease a fireproof dish and put in a layer of cooked rice. Add a few flakes of butter or margarine, some grated cheese and a few grains of cayenne pepper. Repeat until the dish is nearly full, then pour in enough milk to come half-way up the sides. Sprinkle the top with plenty of buttered crumbs, mixed with cheese if you like, and bake until the cheese is melted and the top browned. The proportion of cheese to use is two ounces to a pint of the rice.

Rice and Peas (Risi e Bisi)

An ancient dish of Italy, the national dish of the Venetians. Stew a chopped onion in a tablespoonful or two of butter with a stick of celery, a handful of chopped parsley and two ounces of lean ham or bacon. Do not let them brown, and after a few minutes add a pound of rice and mix well together, cooking on until the rice is a light gold colour, stirring all the while.

Then add by degrees enough boiling stock nearly to cover the rice, and then add the peas from five pounds of pods, season with salt and pepper, and cook gently on a low heat until the rice is tender and has absorbed nearly all the liquid. Just before serving, stir in some grated Parmesan cheese to taste.

Rice and Tomato Pie

Cook a quarter of a pound of rice in a pint of well-flavoured stock, seasoning with salt, pepper and a little curry powder. Peel and slice a pound or so of tomatoes and put these and the rice in alternate layers in a greased fireproof dish. Sprinkle the top with buttered crumbs, and bake for half an hour in a moderate oven. Sprinkle with chopped parsley on serving. If liked, a little grated cheese could be sprinkled between the layers, and also mixed with the breadcrumbs on top.

Riston Rice

Cook half a medium-sized chopped cabbage with two rashers of finely chopped fat bacon over a low heat for half an hour, then add a breakfastcupful and a half of boiled and dried rice, salt, pepper, half a teaspoonful of chopped parsley and a teacupful of veal or chicken stock. Cook on for another quarter of an hour, and serve.

Savoury Rice Roquettes

Steam a teacupful of rice with a teacupful of water seasoned with a level teaspoonful of salt until the water is absorbed, then add a breakfast-cupful of scalded milk, stir lightly with a fork, and steam on until the rice is soft. Add three teaspoonfuls of tomato ketchup or purée and a quarter of a level teaspoonful of paprika pepper, and after it has cooled slightly, stir in two egg-yolks and three level teaspoonfuls of butter or margarine. Spread on a plate to get cold, then cut into appropriate shapes, egg-and-bread-crumb them and fry them.

Pilaff of Lobster, Crab or other Shellfish

This is made by lining a pudding-basin with Pilaff Rice (page 14), and filling the middle with the cooked shellfish bound with a thick suitable sauce, e.g. tomato or cheese or something more savoury and delicious such as a *Sauce Américaine*, covering it with a top layer of the rice and making it hot all through. Turn it out to serve, and pour round the base some of the same sauce that you used to bind the fish, thinning it a little with some of the stock with which it was made.

Louisiana Shrimp

Cook a level teaspoonful of chopped onion in three level dessertspoonfuls of butter for five minutes, stirring all the time, then add two-thirds of a breakfastcupful of picked or tinned shrimps, the same quantity of hot boiled and well-drained rice and the same of thick cream. Heat through, season with half a level teaspoonful of salt, a quarter of a level teaspoonful of celery salt and, if you like, two level tablespoonfuls of tomato ketchup and a few grains of cayenne pepper. Serve very hot. When thick cream is impossible, a very passable imitation can be made by using a thin creamy white sauce instead.

Onions stuffed with Rice

Medium-sized onions can be parboiled, their centres scooped-out, stuffed with savoury rice, and then baked or braised and served in a rich brown gravy or tomato sauce.

Tomatoes stuffed with Rice

Tomatoes make a very handsome dish if they are scooped out, stuffed with a savoury rice or cooked rice mixed with cheese, and then baked in the oven until the top of the stuffing is lightly browned. If the rice has not been prepared already beforehand, the scooped out contents of the tomatoes can be used to add flavour in cooking the rice.

Uncooked tomatoes, hollowed out in the same way, and stuffed with cold savoury rice make a delicious light cold luncheon dish.

Turnips stuffed with Rice

See *Turnips stuffed with Semolina* on page 51, using savoury rice for the stuffing instead.

MACARONI and SPAGHETTI

THESE two Italian pastes are made from a specially " hard " wheat, rich in gluten and unsuitable for making bread, which is grown on poor soils originally in Italy and Southern Russia. The difference between them is that macaroni is tubular and made in various sizes, while spaghetti is in long solid strings about twice the thickness of the smallest paste of this kind, vermicelli, which is used only in milk puddings or as a garnish for clear soups and broths with which we need not be concerned here.

Although both these pastes are usually bought dried in packets, they can be obtained freshly made in Soho, and the enterprising reader is urged to try the fresh against the dried, if possible, when the difference in flavour and texture will be a revelation.

There are many ways of garnishing both these pastes which will pleasantly surprise those whose knowledge of them is confined to macaroni cheese, and these will be found in the ensuing pages.

Macaroni and Spaghetti

The preliminary cooking of these pastes requires a little attention. The first essential is to see that they have plenty of water to cook in, the water should be salted, and it should be on the full boil when the paste is put into it. When macaroni is in long strips these should not be broken, but slipped into the water by one end. The boiling water will soften it, and you will find that the rest of the length slides in quite easily on its own, or at any rate with a little gentle help. The actual cooking will not take longer than five to twelve or fifteen minutes for dried macaroni, according to the length of time it has been kept, while home-made pastes like *tagliatelle* will need only a few minutes.

These pastes should not be overcooked, and when they are done they should still feel slightly firm between the teeth. Nor should they stick together. Each strand should be quite separate from the others, and this can be ensured by draining them thoroughly in a colander after they are cooked, and running a little hot water over them to remove superfluous starch. If you do not use enough water or if you cook the paste too long, you are only asking for disappointment.

Macaroni Alla Marinara

Mix the cooked macaroni with tomato sauce in which one or two tablespoonfuls of capers and a few stoned olives have been included.

Macaroni Alla Napolitana

Cook three-quarters of a pound of macaroni, and put it into a saucepan with half a pint of white sauce, half a pint of tomato sauce, three or four ounces of grated Parmesan cheese, half a dozen lightly fried sliced mushrooms and half an ounce of cooked tongue cut in very small pieces. Toss over a good heat for ten minutes or so, stirring all the time, and serve very hot.

Macaroni Alla Toranese

Mix lightly browned dice of bacon and fried sliced onions, both bound with a little butter, with the cooked and drained macaroni.

Macaroni and Onions

Cook some macaroni and make a white sauce with milk and some of the water in which the macaroni was cooked, seasoning it well with salt, pepper, a bay leaf and a little nutmeg or mace. Meanwhile chop up some spring onions and fry them tender in a little butter or margarine, add them to the sauce with the fat they were fried in and simmer together for about twenty minutes. Then add the drained macaroni to the sauce, and either heat well through and serve with grated cheese handed separately, or pour the mixture into a shallow fireproof dish, sprinkle the top with cheese and brown quickly in the oven or under the grill.

Macaroni and Tomatoes

Cook half a pound of macaroni. Grease a baking-dish, and put in a layer of the macaroni, then a layer of stewed or tinned tomatoes seasoned with salt and pepper, then another layer of macaroni, and so on. When the dish is nearly full, sprinkle well with grated cheese and then with breadcrumbs, add a few flakes of butter or margarine, and bake in the oven for twenty minutes to half an hour, until the top is nicely browned.

Macaroni Bolognese

Drain the cooked macaroni well, pour over it plenty of the *Ragu Sauce Bolognese* described below, and sprinkle with grated Parmesan cheese. Put half a pound of lean raw beef and four ounces of streaky green bacon through the mincing-machine with an onion, a carrot and a stick of celery, and brown all these in two ounces of butter or margarine, seasoning with salt and pepper and adding one or two cloves. Then moisten with half a pint of stock or water, simmer for twenty minutes, then add another half-pint of the liquid and a level tablespoonful of tomato sauce or purée. Then barely cover the contents of the pan with stock or water, bring to the boil and simmer for about two hours. Just before serving stir in a quarter of a pint of cream.

Macaroni Italienne

Toss the macaroni, after cooking, with a little butter, cream and grated cheese, seasoning it with salt and pepper.

Macaroni Languedocienne

First in a frying-pan fry in olive oil three peeled aubergines (or egg-plants) cut in slices, and six sliced tomatoes, seasoned with chopped garlic, salt, pepper and a sprig of thyme. When they are done, drain them, and add to the liquid of their cooking a few cut-up mushrooms. Add these to the aubergines and tomatoes. Now toss some cooked macaroni in butter, and after seasoning it put it into a shallow dish, sprinkle it with grated cheese, and cover it with the stewed vegetables.

Macaroni Niçoise (1)

This is prepared in the first instance as *Macaroni Italienne*, but there are added as well some chopped onion lightly fried in olive oil, a touch of garlic and some roughly chopped cooked tomatoes.

Macaroni Niçoise (2)

As above, but add as well a little purée of anchovies or even a few drops of anchovy essence.

Macaroni with Anchovies

For this Provençal dish first cook in a saucepan half a dozen unsalted anchovies with four ounces of butter, but do not let them boil. Mash them up and add four or five spoonfuls of tomato purée, and then put in your macaroni, already cooked and well drained. Mix together and serve, handing grated cheese separately.

Macaroni with Shrimp Sauce

Make a thick white sauce flavoured with anchovy essence and seasoned with salt and pepper, and to half a pint of this add half a pint of picked shrimps. Pour this over half a pound of cooked macaroni already waiting in a hot dish.

Macaroni with Tomato

Toss the cooked macaroni with tomato sauce to which you have added some chopped fried onion, and sprinkle generously with grated cheese.

French Macaroni

This is highly unusual and should be tried. Cut six rolls in halves, and pour a little red wine in the middle of each half, using about half a pint of wine in all. Let them soak for an hour, and then cook a quarter of a pound of macaroni, drain it, mix it in a saucepan with an ounce of butter, and then stir in six ounces of grated cheese. Mix well together, heap over the rolls, sprinkle with a little grated nutmeg and brown in a hot oven for ten minutes.

Neapolitan Macaroni

Boil half a pound of macaroni for ten minutes only, drain it and put it into a saucepan with a quarter of a pint of dry white wine and an eighth of a pint of fish stock. Add a chopped onion and six chopped anchovy fillets first fried in butter or margarine until the onion is tender, and simmer all together for twenty minutes. Then serve in a hot dish with some grated cheese sprinkled on top.

Savoury Macaroni

Boil a quarter of a pound of macaroni, and while it is cooking fry half a pound of sliced onions in a little butter or margarine. Then mix the drained macaroni and onions together adding a tablespoonful of dried sage and salt and pepper to taste. When cooled, add three eggs beaten in two tablespoonfuls of milk, turn into a greased pie-dish, and bake for an hour.

This may be varied by the inclusion in the mixture of a tablespoonful or two of chopped bacon or ham.

Virginia Macaroni

This is a little different from the usual macaroni cheese and is perhaps worth including:

Cook and drain half a pound of macaroni, and put half of it in a greased baking-dish. Sprinkle with half a teacupful of grated cheese and half a level teaspoonful of dry mustard. Dot with butter or margarine, and repeat the layers once. Pour in two breakfastcupfuls of not too thick white sauce, sprinkle with a teacupful of buttered crumbs, and bake in a hot oven until the top is browned.

Spaghetti Sicilienne

Fry half a pound of chopped onions crisply in a little suitable fat, and then add two chopped cloves of garlic, four rashers of bacon cut in fair sized pieces, a quarter of a pound of sliced mushrooms, four cut up anchovies in oil, a handful of chopped parsley and about a dozen stoned black olives. Cook together for a few minutes. Put about three-quarters of a pound of cooked spaghetti into a dish with a little olive oil and toss it together, then pile up the vegetable mixture on top, and serve as hot as possible, with a dish of grated Parmesan cheese handed separately.

Spaghetti with Eggs

Put into a greased fireproof dish alternate layers of cooked spaghetti, skinned and sliced tomatoes and sliced hard-boiled eggs. When the dish is nearly full, pour in a creamy Béchamel sauce flavoured with grated cheese, sprinkle the top with more cheese, and bake in a moderate oven until the top is golden-brown.

Spaghetti with Garlic Sauce

Something for the hardened garlic-addict! For dressing half a pound of cooked and drained spaghetti, heat up half a teacupful of olive oil with two or three split cloves of garlic. Then take out the garlic, toss the spaghetti in the oil and serve at once. This can be varied by adding to the spaghetti, just before you mix it with the oil, half a dozen anchovy fillets in oil, cut in small pieces. Warmed black olives would be pleasant enough with this.

Spaghetti with Mushrooms

Toss the spaghetti in oil flavoured with garlic as above, and add a teacupful to a breakfast-cupful of sliced and fried mushrooms.

Spaghetti with Clams

An odd American variation to be made with tinned clams, is to add to the spaghetti prepared as above, a teacupful of chopped drained tinned clams. There is no reason why these should not be replaced by tinned oysters.

NOODLES

NOODLES are perhaps one of the most ancient forms of food still to be found upon our tables, originating in China many centuries ago and said to have been introduced into Europe by the famous Venetian traveller, Marco Polo, in the twelfth century. In that country noodles are now known as *tagliatelle*, and from thence this charming form of ribbon paste spread to Southern Germany, where it was called *nudeln*, and thence to France and Western Europe under the name of *nouilles*. Like macaroni, noodles can be bought ready dried, but unlike macaroni, they can be quite easily made at home, and benefit very greatly by being cooked when freshly made. The reader is therefore recommended to try a hand at home in preparation and to experiment with the recipe set out below:

Noodles or Tagliatelle

To make this delicious ribbon macaroni is simple in the extreme. Work three-quarters of a pound of flour to a paste with three whole eggs and one yolk, adding a pinch of salt. When it is quite firm and smooth, roll out thinly into two or three sheets of paste, and let these stand for about twenty minutes or longer to get dry. Then put the sheet of pastry on a floured board, and roll it up like a roly-poly. Cut it now downwards into quarter-inch strips, unroll these and spread them out on a floured cloth to dry again. That is all. They are made in various widths in different parts of Europe, but generally about a quarter of an inch is about right. They are cooked in boiling stock or salted water, and when freshly made will take about three or four minutes to be ready.

If they are made the day before, they will take a little longer, and if they are bought ready dried, they will need the same length of cooking as macaroni or spaghetti.

Noodles Alsacienne

When the noodles are cooked and drained, put them into a shallow dish, sprinkle them with coarse browned breadcrumbs, and pour over them some butter which you have just heated to the flaming stage.

Or take a third of the cooked noodles, fry them golden in a little butter. Then just toss the rest in more butter, put them into a dish and sprinkle the fried ones on top.

Noodles with Anchovies and Tunny Fish

Heat two ounces of butter or margarine in a saucepan with four tablespoonfuls of olive oil, and add four ounces of tunny fish in oil (nowadays Americanized into Tuna Fish) finely chopped and two or three anchovies chopped as well. Mix together and cook for a few minutes, then add, off the heat, a tablespoonful of chopped parsley, a little pepper and three or four tablespoonfuls of grated Parmesan cheese. Pour over the cooked noodles, stir together and serve.

Noodles with Bacon

Stew three tablespoonfuls of diced bacon in a little butter, and add half a pound of cooked and drained noodles. Mix together, stir in a tablespoonful of grated cheese, and serve as hot as possible.

Noodles with Cheese

Drain half a pound of cooked noodles, melt some butter in a frying-pan but do not let it brown. Put in the noodles, and toss them in the butter with a spoon and fork until they are coated with it all over. Put them into a hot serving-dish, sprinkle them with grated cheese, and toss them together again in the same way until the cheese melts. It is important that this last operation be done in the dish, as we do not want to cook the cheese, as we should do if we tossed it in the pan.

Noodles with Liver

Mince half a pound of cooked calf's liver, and fry a chopped onion golden-brown in butter or margarine. Mix both these with half a pound of cooked and well drained noodles, turn all into a greased fireproof dish, and bake in a moderate oven until golden-brown on top.

Noodles with Mushrooms

Stew four sliced mushrooms in six table-spoonfuls of butter for five minutes, then add half a pound of cooked noodles. Season with salt and pepper, and if you like a little nutmeg, toss all together until well heated through. The pan may be first advantageously rubbed round with a cut clove of garlic.

Noodles with Spinach

Cook and drain half a pound of noodles. Heat up some minced, cooked or tinned and well drained spinach in a little butter, with a teaspoonful of sugar and salt and pepper to taste. Mix the noodles with this and serve, adding a touch of grated nutmeg if you wish. Grated cheese could be mixed with this dish or handed separately.

Fried Noodles

Cook half a pound of noodles, and when they are done drain and dry them in a cloth. Now brown them delicately in three level tablespoonfuls of butter or margarine, and serve them sprinkled with tiny dice of fried bread.

Savoury Noodles

This is a famous American dish. Melt two ounces of butter or other suitable fat, and fry in it four large sliced onions and three-quarters of a pound of sausage meat. If the sausage meat is known to be fat, very little butter will be needed as the onions will fry in the sausage fat. When both are well browned, add a breakfastcupful of water mixed with sufficient tomato purée to make a thick sauce, half a pound of peeled and sliced mushrooms, some diced celery, two green sweet peppers (when possible) cut up finely, salt, pepper, the juice of a quarter of a lemon and half a pound of white cheese cut in small pieces. Simmer together for a quarter of an hour, then add your cooked and drained noodles, mix them in, cover closely and cook on slowly for another hour.

Noodle Balls

Roll out some noodle paste thinly, fold it in two and cut it out into circles about half an inch in diameter. Plunge these into hot fat in a frying-basket, and fry for two minutes, when they will have swollen into light brown-coloured little balls. Drain and serve sprinkled with grated cheese.

Spinach Noodles

(See *Green Tagliatelle* below)

If you go into some of the provision shops in Soho, you will find different kinds of pastes, of varying shapes and sizes, coloured either green or red. The red ones are coloured with tomato purée and the green ones with spinach, and here is a recipe which shows how to make those sorts coloured green.

Green Tagliatelle

Take enough cooked or tinned sieved spinach, well drained, to give you a handful. When it is as dry as possible, rub it through a sieve, and press it once more between the hands to remove as much moisture as you can. Work this in with the flour and egg in the *Tagliatelle* recipe on page 38, allowing a little longer for it to dry, since the spinach gives the paste extra moisture. When cut in ribbons and cooked, mix it with one of your tomato sauces, and add a few table-spoonfuls of grated cheese. You must, of course, use the bright green tinned spinach for this, and not the strange-looking olive-green stuff that emerges from some tins, for in the green colour contrasting with the red sauce lies much of the charm of this unusual but easily prepared dish.

Tagliatelle alla Romagnola

Brown a clove of garlic and a handful of chopped parsley in olive oil, and then add six or seven tomatoes sliced, and a seasoning of salt and pepper. Strain off the sauce when the tomatoes are cooked, and use this to pour over the cooked tagliatelle, adding a little butter or margarine and a sprinkling of grated Parmesan cheese and serving at once.

Tagliatelle Bolognese

Boil and drain half a pound of *tagliatelle* Heat an ounce and a half of butter or margarine. in a frying-pan and fry in it until a light golden colour two ounces of coarsely chopped ham. Then add the *tagliatelle*, mix together and cook on for a minute or two, and then stir in an ounce of grated Parmesan cheese to serve.

RAVIOLI

OF the many various kinds of stuffed pastes to be found in Italy, *agnellotti, anolini, cannelloni,* and so on, those named *Ravioli* are best known in this country and indeed all over the world. Simple to make and susceptible of a number of savoury fillings, they are admirable for a main course in a light meal. A few selections are given below:

Ravioli

There are several ways of making the paste for these delicious trifles and that in more general use is the paste already described under *Noodles* on page 38. It can, however, be made with two whole eggs and one yolk to a pound of flour, with three or four tablespoonfuls of olive oil and enough water to make a similarly stiff paste. The paste is worked well, and then left to stand for about half an hour, and then cut into three-inch rounds. Various fillings will be found below, and a little of the chosen mixture is placed in the middle of a round of the paste, another round is put on top, and the edges wetted and pinched well down so that they stick together, They are then poached in salted water for eight to ten minutes, and served either with melted butter and grated cheese or in gravy or tomato sauce or the Bolognese sauce described on page 31.

Ravioli Stuffing (1)

(American)

Mix together half a teacupful of cracker biscuit crumbs, a teacupful of grated Parmesan cheese, half a teacupful of chopped cooked or tinned spinach, salt, pepper, a slightly beaten egg and chicken stock to moisten.

Ravioli Stuffing (2)

Fry three-quarters of a pound of calf's liver with two sliced onions, and then put both through the mincing-machine. Mix them with a minced anchovy fillet and a quarter of a pound of minced spinach. Season with salt and pepper, and bind with a beaten egg.

Ravioli Stuffing (3)

Mix together three and a half ounces of fine brown breadcrumbs, two ounces of grated Parmesan cheese and a teaspoonful of chopped onion, season with nutmeg and bind with two or three teaspoonfuls of melted meat glaze and a beaten egg.

Ravioli Alla Romana

Both the paste and the stuffing for these is slightly different from those given above, the paste being made with ten ounces of flour, two eggs, a pinch of salt and a little water. The stuffing is made by mixing ten ounces of sour milk cheese with an egg, a pinch of salt and a tablespoonful of grated Parmesan cheese, and the *ravioli* are boiled in plenty of salted water, and served with melted butter and grated cheese or with a gravy which is made in the same way as the Bolognese sauce on page 31, with the omission of the cream.

SEMOLINA

SEMOLINA is made from the same sort of " hard " wheat that is used in the manufacture of macaroni and the other Italian pastes, but I cannot agree with André Simon in his " Concise Encyclopaedia of Gastronomy " that its nourishing and digestive qualities are " chiefly valuable in the nursery, as pappy food for infants ", although our earliest encounters with it in childhood have generally been in the form of Semolina Pudding.

It is principally famous, of course, in restaurants, in the form of *Gnocchi*, one of the best of all cheese dishes, and there are other highly pleasant ways of using it, as the following pages will endeavour to show.

Gnocchi Alla Romana

This, in my opinion, is the supreme manifestation of semolina, and although *gnocchi* can be made with flour or even mashed potato, those made with semolina remain my favourite. For a large dish, you must boil up a quart of milk, and shower into it while it is boiling half a pound of semolina. Stir all the time with a wooden spoon to prevent lumps, and go on stirring for about ten minutes until the mixture thickens. Then, off the heat, stir in two tablespoonfuls of grated Parmesan cheese, an ounce and a half of butter or margarine, two egg-yolks and a good pinch of salt. Mix evenly, and then spread out, about half an inch thick, on a dish first rinsed with cold water, and leave it for a couple of hours or so to get quite cold. Then cut it into squares or rounds about an inch in diameter, and fill a shallow fireproof dish with alternate layers of these and grated cheese. Sprinkle the top layer with more grated cheese, and pour over all a couple of ounces of melted butter or margarine, Brown the whole thing lightly in a hot oven for about a quarter of an hour, and serve at once.

Gnocchi Flan

Make a fairly large cooked pastry flan, and fill it with cooked *gnocchi*. Pour a creamy cheese sauce over them, sprinkle the top with grated cheese and heat through in the oven to brown the cheese lightly.

Semolina and Cheese Pie

Sprinkle two ounces of semolina into a pint of heated milk, stir until the mixture boils and then simmer gently for ten minutes. Now off the fire add two ounces of grated cheese, seasoned with salt, pepper and half a teaspoonful of made mustard, and mix all well together. Turn into a greased fireproof dish, cover the top with half a pound of skinned and sliced tomatoes, and sprinkle another ounce of grated cheese on top of these. Then bake in a quick oven for about twenty minutes, until the top is lightly browned.

Semolina Croquettes

Put half a pint of milk and half an ounce of butter or margarine into a saucepan, and when boiling shower in, stirring, an ounce of semolina. Cook slowly for ten minutes, then cool a little and add a yolk and a half of egg and half an ounce of grated cheese. Mix, stir and cook a few minutes longer, then spread the mixture on a dish, and when cold cut into suitable shapes, egg-and-breadcrumb them and fry them golden in deep fat. Serve them garnished with fried parsley, and hand a tomato sauce separately.

Semolina with Bacon

Cook a quarter of a pound of semolina in a pint of milk for ten minutes to a quarter of an hour, then season with salt, pepper and mixed herbs or onion juice and when cool, beat in an egg. Spread the mixture on a rinsed plate, and when cold, cut in rounds about an inch thick, Arrange these in a fireproof dish alternately with rashers of streaky bacon, cover the top with breadcrumbs and sprinkle with melted butter or margarine, and brown lightly in the oven.

Tomatoes stuffed with Semolina

Baked tomatoes can be very happily stuffed with semolina flavoured with cheese in the same way as the rice-stuffed tomatoes on page 26.

Turnips stuffed with Semolina

Peel some medium-sized turnips, and boil them whole until they are tender. Then scoop out the middles and stuff the hollow with semolina first cooked in stock and flavoured with cheese or with the turnip purée from the centres mixed with a little cooked semolina to thicken it. Now sprinkle each stuffed turnip with a little cheese or cheese and breadcrumbs, and bake them in a fireproof dish in a hot oven for about a quarter of an hour just to colour the tops. A thick brown sauce or gravy should be poured round them on serving.

Baked or braised *Onions* can be stuffed in the same way.

HARICOT BEANS

LITTLE need be said of the dried bean which has become a feature of English cooking, whether it is the small haricot of which the American Navy Bean is an example, or the larger pallid butter bean which in my opinion has little to be said for it beside its smaller cousin. But for many years the tinned haricot bean in tomato sauce has contributed so monotonously to our meals that it may be a comfort to find other ways of eating them, if only to make our own pot of Boston Beans which are so very much nicer than the commercial article. All these beans have their satisfying qualities, and it would be a pity not to make a somewhat more imaginative use of them.

Haricot Beans

In most cases these beans have to be cooked before they undergo further preparation, and it may be worth while giving here what I have found out to be the only really satisfactory way of doing this, and of preventing that hardness and bitterness of flavour that is only too common. Of course, I cannot guarantee that this method will satisfactorily revivify beans which have been kept inordinately long in the grocer's shop, but it will do something at any rate to mitigate their unpleasantness.

Soak the beans not all night, but for three or four hours only, Then drain them and put them into a saucepan with some *tepid* water, which should cover them well. Put the pan on the lowest possible heat, and let the beans very slowly come to the boil, but before they actually boil and when they show signs that boiling will soon begin, take the pan off the heat and leave the beans to get cold in the liquid. By that time they will be seen to have swollen considerably, and the water in the pan (which will be found to have a somewhat unpleasant smell) must be poured away, and fresh, slightly salted boiling water must now be poured over them, enough to cover. Bring to the boil again, and add a carrot cut in four, a bouquet of parsley, thyme and bay leaf, an onion stuck with two or three cloves and, if you like the flavour, add a clove of garlic. Bring the beans just on boiling point again (they must not actually boil if you can help it), then cook them very gently on top of the stove or in a slow oven for an hour and a half to two hours, until they are quite tender. Then drain them, and keep the liquor for making soup. If your water is hard, a pinch of bicarbonate of soda may be added with the last water. And don't believe what some cookery books say about salt hardening the beans. I don't believe it, and its presence certainly adds to the flavour when their cooking is over.

Baked Haricot Beans

Stew two chopped onions and two table-spoonfuls of minced celery in four ounces of butter or margarine, but do not let them brown. Put a layer of cooked haricot beans, using a pound in all, into a greased casserole, and then add a layer of the vegetables, sprinkling each layer with salt and pepper. Repeat the layers until the beans and vegetables are finished, then pour in enough water just to cover the beanf. Sprinkle the top with a tablespoonful of flour browned in the oven, cover with flakes of butter or margarine, and bake slowly for about four hours, until the beans are soft but not mashed up at all.

Boston Baked Beans

This is the famous American dish. Soak a pint of small haricot beans overnight, drain them cover them with fresh water, heat up, slowly and cook very gently until the skins will burst. (To find out when they are ready to do this, take out one or two, blow on them and if they are sufficiently done, the skins will break.) Then drain them and keep the liquor aside. Now blanch a quarter of a pound piece of pickled pork or mild bacon, and put it into the bottom of an earthenware casserole or bean-pot (a two-quart size being the right one), and put the beans over it,   Bring the bean water to the boil, and add a breakfastcup of it to a level teaspoonful of salt, a teacupful or less of treacle and three level teaspoonfuls of sugar mixed with half a level teaspoonful of dry mustard.   Pour this over the beans, and add enough water to cover them.   Put on the lid closely and bake in a slow oven from six to eight hours, adding more water if necessary during the cooking.

Curried Haricot Beans

Mix these when cooked with the *Curry Sauce* given on page 11.   To my mind they make too substantial a dish if accompanied by the usual rice, and I suggest that they should be eaten cold, with a garnish of watercress leaves.

Haricot Bean Pie

Cook half a pound of haricot beans, rub them through a sieve and mix them with two ounces of butter, four ounces of bread crumbs and, when cool, with three beaten eggs, adding a little milk if the mixture looks too stiff. Season with salt, pepper and chopped parsley, turn into a greased baking-dish and bake in a moderate oven for three-quarters of an hour. Serve with tomato sauce or a rich thick brown gravy.

Haricot Beans and Bacon

Cook the soaked haricot beans with a small piece of bacon, and when they are done, serve them mixed with a little tomato sauce and chopped onion lightly fried in margarine or butter. Add if you like a little of the bacon finely chopped, and eat this pleasant mixture with new potatoes and French beans.

Haricot Beans au Gratin

Cook the beans in the usual way, and when they are done mix them with a thickish thin gravy or tomato sauce. Then pour it all into a lightly greased fireproof dish, first rubbed with a cut clove of garlic if you like, and sprinkle them well with browned breadcrumbs. Scatter a few thin flakes of margarine or butter over the crumbs, and bake or grill until the top is well browned.

Haricot Beans Basquaise

When the beans are cooked and drained, add to the pan two sardines first pounded with a little butter or margarine and a little very finely minced shallot or onion. Mix well together so that this savoury butter melts, add salt and pepper and one or two sliced pickled gherkins, shake all together over the heat and turn into a hot dish. Now put a teacupful of the beans' cooking liquor into the pan, add a teaspoonful of vinegar, boil up together, pour over the beans, and serve them garnished with strips or triangles of fried bread.

Haricot Beans Bretonne

Parboil a breakfastcupful and a half of soaked haricot beans, drain them and put them into an earthenware casserole or stewpan. Add a finely chopped onion, half a dozen sweet red peppers rubbed through a sieve, two cloves of finely chopped garlic, a breakfastcupful of strained stewed or tinned tomatoes, two or three ounces of butter or margarine, a breakfastcupful of veal or chicken stock, and two level teaspoonfuls of salt. Mix together, cover tightly, and cook in a slow oven until the beans have absorbed nearly all the sauce.

Haricot Beans Espagnole

Cook the beans in the usual way, adding to the water a clove or two of garlic, a bouquet of parsley, thyme and bay leaf, and some whole mixed spices and peppercorns tied in a muslin bag. Add, too, a spoonful or two of olive oil. When they are done, drain them, and serve them with a little of the cooking liquor poured over them.

Haricot Beans Lyonnaise

Fry some chopped onion in butter or margarine until lightly browned (as for Lyonnaise potatoes), then add the cooked and drained beans and toss together until the beans are slightly browned, serving with a sprinkling of chopped parsley and, if you like, a final squeeze of lemon.

Haricot Beans Provençale

Cook the soaked haricot beans with a little olive oil, two quartered onions, a little bacon cut in dice, a whole clove of garlic and a seasoning of salt and pepper. After tossing them together for a few minutes, moisten with good stock, add a large sliced tomato, and a bouquet consisting of parsley, thyme, bay leaf, two sage leaves and a small sprig of rosemary, and cook gently until the beans are tender. Serve sprinkled with chopped parsley, but before doing this, stir in if you like a little anchovy butter.

Haricot Beans Toscana

When the beans are cooked and drained, turn them on to a hot dish, season them with salt and pepper, toss them in some olive oil and finish with a squeeze of lemon juice.

Butter Beans Fermière

Put two breakfastcupfuls of soaked butter beans into a saucepan and season them with half a level teaspoonful of salt and an eighth of a level teaspoonful of pepper. Now brown a small sliced onion and a teacupful of carrot cut in small dice in some bacon fat, and add this to the beans. Dot over with a few flakes of butter or margarine, add enough water to come half-way up the beans, put on the lid closely, and cook in a slow oven until the beans are soft.

Butter Beans with Tomato Sauce

Cook three-quarters of a pound of soaked butter beans until tender, and while they are cooking brown two chopped onions with three peeled, cored and thinly sliced apples in a little olive oil. When the onions are tender, add half a pint of tomato purée diluted with a little water if too thick, and cook on for another ten minutes or so, stirring. Finally, season with a little salt and lemon juice, and serve the beans mixed with this fragrant sauce.

DRIED PEAS AND LENTILS

THESE two pleasant forms of dried vegetables, like haricot beans, need a little brightening up on our tables, and here are some ways of doing this. And in making the following suggestions, it may be worth while suggesting to the enquiring reader that an eye should be kept open for the little bright green Italian dried peas, *piselli verde*, which are well worth taking some trouble to find.

Lentils (Dahl)

Having removed any stones from half a pound of lentils, soak them for about an hour in cold water, then drain them and put them to boil in warm water with salt and half a teaspoonful of powdered turmeric. Cook them until they are tender, and meanwhile fry a small sliced onion in half an ounce of butter or margarine with half a teaspoonful each of black pepper and paprika pepper. Add this mixture carefully, when the onion is cooked, to the lentils, and stir until you have the consistence of porridge. Then serve.

A drier version of this and, to my mind, a more pleasant one, is made thus. Chop two small onions and fry them nicely brown in two ounces of butter or margarine. Take them out and in the same fat fry half a pound of well-drained soaked lentils. Add a teaspoonful of powdered turmeric, two or three bay leaves and, if you like it hotly seasoned, a teaspoonful of powdered chillies, which I leave out myself, Pour in enough warm water to cover the lentils, put on the lid and let the lentils cook. When they are half-done, add a small green apple, peeled and quartered, and a little more water if it looks as though it wants it. When the lentils are soft and the water absorbed, it is ready to be served garnished with the fried onions that you have set aside.

Curried Lentils

Fry some chopped onion and a little garlic in a little butter or margarine until golden, then add a breakfastcupful of soaked and well drained lentils and fry on for a minute or two, stirring the while. Add curry powder to your taste, cover and leave to mellow on the side of the stove for about ten minutes. Then season with salt and celery salt, and pour in enough stock mixed with some tomato juice or purée to cover the lentils by an inch. Bring to the boil, and cook with the lid on in a slowish oven until the lentils are soft and the stock absorbed. Finish with a few drops of lemon juice.

Lentil and Egg Curry

Boil some eggs hard, shell them, prick them all over with a fork and roll them in curry powder mixed with a little salt. Now fry them gently in two ounces of butter or margarine in a saucepan for about five minutes, then take them out and in the same fat fry a small sliced onion golden-brown. Add a tablespoonful of curry powder and fry on with the onions until a rich brown, add half a pound of well-drained soaked lentils, and cook on for another five minutes. Then add a quarter of a pint of warm water and let the curry simmer until the lentils are done and the water absorbed. Serve with the eggs on top, garnished with more fried onion.

Lentil and Rice Khichri

Put half a pound of rice and half a pint of soaked lentils into a saucepan with a few peppercorns and cloves, one or two bay leaves, and a small piece of root ginger, with salt to taste, and pour in enough water to cover the contents by about an inch. Cover closely and cook in the usual way, very gently, until the rice and lentils are done and the water is all absorbed. Eat it by itself with some mango chutney or use it, if you prefer, as an accompaniment to vegetable curries.

Lentil and Rice Croquettes

Boil four ounces of soaked lentils until tender, and cook the same quantity of rice. Chop up an onion and one or two cloves of garlic very finely, and mix them with the rice and lentils, adding salt and pepper and some dried mixed herbs. When cooling, mix in a beaten egg-yolk. Shape into croquettes when cold, brush over with white of egg, roll in breadcrumbs, and fry golden in deep fat. Serve with a parsley sauce.

Pease Croquettes

Any pease pudding mixture can be bound with an egg-yolk, rolled into croquettes with floured hands, brushed over with egg-white and rolled in crumbs, then fried golden in deep fat. Serve sprinkled with grated cheese or in a brown or tomato sauce.

Savoury Pease Pudding

Soak a pound of split peas overnight, then tie them in a cloth and cook them slowly for about two hours until tender. Now chop up a pared root of celeriac with two onions and the white part of a leek, and brown and stew them in butter or margarine until soft. Mix these with the peas, adding salt and pepper, put the mixture into a greased fireproof dish, and bake in a moderate oven for an hour. This is good with a tomato sauce poured over it, though an onion sauce would be good too, though not so decorative.

SWEET CORN

IT is not very many years ago when sweet or maize corn was practically unknown in this country, except in tins, but now quick-growing varieties suitable for our peculiar climate have been developed and now there are few greengrocers' shops which do not sport the milky cobs in the late summer. Corn-on-the-Cob is a dish in itself, but there are a great many ways of preparing this delicious vegetable, whether fresh, quick-frozen or tinned, A few follow:

Sweet Corn

As some of the recipes that follow demand cooked fresh corn, here is the proper way to cook it. Use only young and tender corn (there is a saying that you can walk up the kitchen garden to cut it, but you must run back to the kitchen with it, for it spoils if it is kept too long before cooking), and first take off the outside husks and as much of the " silk " as possible. Put the cobs thus prepared into a pan of boiling *unsalted* water, and boil them rapidly from twenty to thirty minutes, according to their size.

Sweet Corn and Tomatoes

Peel and chop up a pound of tomatoes, put them into a stewpan with salt, pepper, a touch of sugar and a little butter or margarine, and stew them gently on a low heat until they have reduced to two-thirds of their original bulk. Meanwhile cook six ears of corn as directed above, strip the grains from the cobs, stir them into the stewed tomatoes and serve with sippets of toast or fried bread.

Barbecued Sweet Corn

Strip the husks and as much " silk " as possible from the young cobs, wrap each up in rashers of not too fat bacon and tie them with thread or fix the bacon in place with skewers. Grill them then *very slowly*, turning them often, so that the bacon cooks evenly.   When it is crisp, the cobs are ready.

Corn Fritters

Drain the contents of a tin of corn, measuring out a breakfastcupful. Chop this up and add a teacupful and a half of flour sieved with half a level teaspoonful of salt, the same of baking powder and a dash of paprika pepper. Add a well-beaten egg-yolk, and lastly fold in the stiffly-beaten egg-white. Fry delicately brown in spoonfuls in deep hot fat.

Serve garnished with fried tomatoes or mushrooms or both.

Corn Oysters

Use the recipe for *Corn Fritters* an page 66, but leave out the baking powder and reduce the flour to half a teacupful. Cook in spoonfuls on a hot griddle or thick frying-pan in bacon fat.

Both the above recipes can be varied by the addition of a little grated cheese to the mixture.

Fried Sweet Corn

Cut the grains from eight young corn cobs, and put these into a heavy frying-pan in which you have first heated a tablespoonful of lard or bacon fat. Add half a teaspoonful of salt and a breakfastcupful of water. Smooth the corn out flat, and brown well on the bottom side. Place a plate or dish over the pan, turn it upside-down, put a little more of the fat into the pan, slide the cake off the plate into it, and brown the other side.

Sweet Corn Timbales

Beat up three eggs with half a pint of milk, and add an eighth of a pint of cream and two ounces of fresh sweet corn scraped from the cob Season with salt and cayenne pepper, and fill some greased timbales cases with the mixture. Steam, covered with greased paper, for twenty minutes to half an hour, then turn them out and serve them with a tomato sauce poured round and over them.

Sweet Corn Toast

Rather good for a quick snackish meal. Cook a teaspoonful of chopped onion in a level tablespoonful and a half of butter or margarine for two or three minutes, stirring all the time, then add a breakfastcupful of drained tinned corn, chopped if you like, some thin cream or creamy milk and a seasoning of salt and paprika pepper. Bring to the boil, simmer for five minutes, then pour over pieces of buttered toast, and serve at once, garnished with crisply fried or baked rolls of streaky bacon.

Scalloped Corn

Cook half an onion, finely chopped, in three level dessertspoonfuls of butter or margarine for five minutes, stirring all the time, and then add two dessertspoonfuls of flour sieved with a level teaspoonful of salt, and quarter of a level teaspoonful each of paprika pepper and dry mustard and a few grains of cayenne pepper, and mix well with the fat. Now, still stirring, add by degrees a teacupful of milk, bring to the boil and add a breakfastcupful of drained tinned sweet corn, the yolk of an egg and a teacupful of stale bread broken in small pieces and well browned in a little butter. Turn into a baking-dish, sprinkle with buttered crumbs, and bake in a hot oven until the crumbs are browned. Any sort of bottled sauce can be added to the mixture if liked, in proportion to taste.

POLENTA

POLENTA, a yellow flour made from maize, is essentially Italian, and provides a staple food in many parts of that country, being eaten even in the form of bread, and this preference is repeated in various districts of the United States. Like other forms of maize or sweet corn, it possesses a distinct and to my mind very attractive flavour of its own, and to those who have not yet sampled it, I can only recommend an instant trial.

Polenta

It is difficult to give exact instructions about cooking *polenta*, since it absorbs varying quantities of water according to its quality, but it is fairly safe to say that the approximate quantities are just under half a pint of water to each half-pound of maize flour. Put the water into a saucepan with a good pinch of salt, then shower in the maize flour (in the same way that we are accustomed to shower in semolina), stirring all the time with a wooden spoon. Then let it cook very slowly, stirring it often, for about half an hour, adding a little more boiling water from time to time if necessary. When it is done, it should be thick and quite smooth, with no lumps in it, and it can be eaten either as it is, with butter and grated cheese handed separately, or the cheese and butter can be stirred into the pan of *polenta* just before it leaves the fire.

In the recipes that follow calling for cold *polenta*, it must be understood that the *polenta* is quite plain, with neither butter nor cheese added to it.

Polenta Bolognese

Cut some cooked *polenta* into thin slices when cold, and put them into a shallow fireproof dish with the *ragu sauce a la Bolognese* on page 31. Heat through in a moderate oven without browning for about a quarter of an hour.

Fried Polenta

Cut slices of cold *polenta*, and brown them lightly in hot olive oil, butter or margarine. Serve with tomato sauce and grated cheese.

Polenta fried with Cheese

Cut some cold *polenta* into thin rounds two inches in diameter, and sprinkle half of these with grated cheese. Press the other round firmly on top, and brush them over with beaten egg-yolk. Then fry them golden on both sides in olive oil or butter or margarine.

Polenta with Tomato and Cheese

Cut the cold *polenta* in squares or rectangles, put them into a fireproof dish, pour a tomato sauce over them, sprinkle them with plenty of grated cheese and brown quickly in the oven.

POTATOES

POTATOES have always been well-known for providing a substantial dish when meat or other comestibles cannot be procured, and this has resulted in a large number of recipes of interest, especially among the nations on the Continent. Some of these will be found here, along with the simpler kinds from our own land. As indicated here and there in the following pages, these potato dishes can be enlivened and adorned by such garnishes as poached or fried eggs or triangles of fried bread, toast or pastry, but for the modest appetite they will be found attractive and satisfying as they are.

Banffshire Potatoes

Peel some potatoes of the same size, cut half an inch off the top, and hollow out the inside of each, leaving a shell of about half an inch all round. (This is not so difficult as it looks, if a thin teaspoon is used.) Fill these with the following mixture. Cream an ounce of butter or margarine, add the yolk of an egg and beat a little longer. Then mix this with three ounces of breadcrumbs, a pinch of mixed herbs, a little chopped parsley, three-quarters of a gill of milk (one gill equals a quarter of a pint), and a seasoning of pepper and salt. Put on the top you have cut off, and bake in a hot oven for an hour.

Devilled Potatoes

Boil some new potatoes, and while they are cooking melt two tablespoonfuls of margarine and add a teaspoonful of made mustard, a tablespoonful of vinegar, a pinch of salt, and a few grains of cayenne pepper, Cook this mixture for three or four minutes, and when the potatoes are done and drained, add them to this sauce with the well-beaten yolks of two eggs. Shake over the heat for a minute or two, and serve at once in a border of boiled or pilaff rice.

Hungarian Potatoes

Fry a quarter of a pound of chopped onions in margarine or lard without browning them, and when they are soft, add a teaspoonful or so of paprika pepper. Now add two or three peeled and sliced tomatoes, and two pounds of peeled and rather thickly sliced raw potatoes, Just cover with stock, and cook in the oven with the lid on until the stock has practically disappeared. Serve sprinkled with chopped parsley.

Pittsburgh Potatoes

Cut some potatoes into one-third inch cubes, and boil a quart measure of these with a finely chopped onion in enough water to cover them, for five minutes from the time the water comes to the boil. Add three tinned red sweet peppers cut in small pieces, and cook for another seven minutes, Drain off the water, and turn the vegetables into a greased baking-dish, pouring over them a pint of cheese sauce. Then bake in a moderate oven until the potatoes are done and the top golden.

Polish Potato Cake

Cook and mash some potatoes well, ready for frying as a large cake in the frying-pan, but before putting the cake into the pan, add to the potatoes a chopped hard-boiled egg and two minced anchovies for each pound of potato. Garnish, if you like, with more hard-boiled egg in quarters or slices, and little anchovy curls or fillets.

Potato and Artichoke Stew

Fry a chopped onion in a little butter or margarine until golden-brown, stir in a tablespoonful of flour, cook for a few minutes, and then moisten with white stock or water. Season with salt, pepper and chopped parsley and then add some peeled and sliced potatoes and Jerusalem artichokes in whatever proportion you wish. Cover closely, and simmer for about thirty-five minutes or until the vegetables are cooked.

Potato and Cheese Cake

Melt a little fat in a frying-pan and line the bottom with thin slices of raw potato, so that they overlap and cover the pan completely. Sprinkle these with plenty of grated cheese and a little salt, and then add another layer of potato slices. Season with salt, cover the pan with a lid or plate and cook on a fairly good heat for about twenty minutes. The bottom layer should then be done, and it must be then turned over (which can be done quite easily by sliding it out on to a plate and then inverting the plate over the pan, and the second side browned. It should then be eaten immediately with a watercress or other green salad.

Potato and Macaroni Pie

Slice some boiled potatoes thinly, and line a greased fireproof dish with them, sprinkling them afterwards with grated cheese. Put a layer of cooked macaroni over the potatoes, then add another of potatoes, sprinkling this with more cheese. Finish with another layer of potatoes, pour a thick tomato sauce over all, scatter some more cheese over this, and brown in the oven.

Potato and Mushroom Pudding

Make some nice mashed potatoes, and bind them with an egg-yolk, flavouring very slightly with lemon juice. Grease a mould or soufflé-case and put the potatoes into it, making a good-sized cavity in the middle for the mushrooms. This should be filled with small cooked mushrooms bound with a white, brown or mushroom sauce. Put a lid of the mashed potato over the top, and bake in a moderate oven for three-quarters of an hour to an hour. Turn it out when done, and serve with a contrasting sauce, such as tomato or cheese.

Potato and Onion Pie

Cut a pound of potatoes and half a pound of onions into dice, chop up a stick of celery and mix them all together. Now toss them in a tablespoonful of margarine, and stew them, covered, for ten minutes, stirring now and again. Put them into a pie-dish, add half a pint of milk or well-flavoured vegetable stock, a tablespoonful of chopped parsley and seasoning to taste, cover with a pastry lid and bake for about forty minutes. Serve hot.

Potato Blanquette

Boil some small new potatoes, and while they are cooking make a white sauce with a tablespoonful of butter or margarine, the same of flour and a good breakfastcupful of white stock or milk or a mixture of both. At the same time cook a few quartered mushrooms in a little fat of the kind used. When the potatoes are done,

drain them well, and add them with the mushrooms to the sauce, which you have bound with
the yolk of an egg.   It will be found an improve-
ment if a little lemon juice is beaten with the
egg-yolk, and some parsley sprinkled over the
dish on serving.

Potato Cheese Fritters

Mash up a pound of boiled potatoes, and
mix them with a tablespoonful of flour, amalga-
mating them well together, four good tablespoonfuls of grated cheese, a seasoning of salt,
pepper and grated nutmeg and a whole egg.
When the mixture has cooled, roll it out, and
cut it into rounds or whatever shapes you fancy.
Fry these golden on both sides in a little fat,
either as they are or first rolled in fine breadcrumbs or oatmeal.

Potato Cheese Squares

Bind some mashed potato with an egg-yolk,
adding a little flour to the potato first if it is
not stiff enough to roll out.   Now cut some
cheese—processed cheese will do well here—
into half-inch cubes, spread each with a little
made mustard, and wrap them up separately in
some of the potato mixture rolled out.   See
that the cheese is well covered, shape into
squares, and leave them for a little while to dry.
Then bake them in a greased tin in a hot oven
for about ten minutes.

Potato Curry

Cook the potatoes in their skins, peel them and cut them in quarters or slices while still hot, and serve them in the curry sauce described on page 11. Potatoes and lentils make a good curry, and hard-boiled egg can also be added, if liked.

Potato Dumplings

Mash two medium-sized potatoes smoothly and mix them with pepper, nutmeg and a beaten egg. Add enough flour to make a fairly stiff dough, and drop spoonfuls of this into boiling stock and cook for ten minutes. Serve them sprinkled with buttered crumbs and grated cheese, or with tiny dice of bread fried in margarine and chopped parsley.

Potato Flan

Make some fairly rich pastry, and roll out two rounds about a quarter of an inch thick. Spread one of them with rounds of raw potato about the size and thickness of a five-shilling piece until you have a layer about an inch high. Season lightly with salt and pepper, and put the other pastry round on top, closing the edges all round after moistening them with a little milk or water. Bake slowly for an hour, then take off the top carefully, pour in as much cream as you can, put on the top again and let the flan get cold. When you want to serve it, heat it up again.

Potato Loaf

Boil an onion with some rice for twenty minutes, then drain the rice, measure out a pint of it and chop up enough of the onion to give two tablespoonfuls. Mix this with a pound of cooked potatoes put through the ricer and bind with two beaten eggs, seasoning with salt and, pepper. Steam in a greased pudding basin for an hour and a half, and then turn it out and pour a tomato or cheese sauce over it to serve.

Potato, Onion and Cheese Mould

Peel and slice thinly a pound and a half of potatoes, slice two or three onions finely, and grate a quarter of a pound of cheese. Grease a pudding-basin or charlotte mould rather thickly, and sprinkle it with browned bread-crumbs, shaking out those that do not stick to the sides. Then fill up with alternate layers of potato, cheese and onion in that order, beginning and ending with potato. Now melt an ounce of margarine in half a pint of hot stock or milk-and-water, season with salt, pepper, and a touch of grated nutmeg, and pour this into the mould. Bake in a moderate oven for an hour and a half, and then turn out carefully. Or prepare the whole thing in a casserole, without the breadcrumbs, and serve it in it.

Potato Pancakes

Grate some raw potato into cold water, drain it well, pressing out as much moisture as you can, and measure out two breakfastcupfuls. Now make a batter with an egg, a couple of tablespoonfuls of flour and a little milk, and season this with salt, pepper and onion juice. Mix the potato into this, and drop spoonfuls into hot fat in a frying-pan. Brown on each side, and serve with sprinkled cheese or with a cheese or some other suitable sauce handed separately.

Potato Pasty

Make half a pound of pastry and roll it out into a large round. Cut some raw potatoes into small dice and do the same to a little turnip and onion, and heap a mixture of these, potato greatly predominating, on one side of the pastry round. Add a little chopped parsley and a flake or two of butter or margarine. Fold over the other pastry half to make a large turnover, and wet and pinch the edges well together. Make a hole in the top, and bake for about an hour in a hot oven until the pastry has set, and then in a moderate one until it is finished. It will take about an hour in all.

Potato Pie

Cut two sticks of celery and two carrots into small dice and two onions in slices, and cook them gently, without browning them, in a little margarine or dripping. Now cut three pounds of potatoes into thick rings, and add them to the other vegetables with a dessertspoonful of chopped parsley and a drop or two of lemon juice. Just cover with boiling stock or hot water, and cook for half an hour with the lid off. Now put it all into a greased fireproof dish, sprinkle the top with grated cheese and breadcrumbs and brown in the oven for a quarter of an hour or so.

Potato Roll

Roll out half a pound of pastry thinly to a rectangle, as for a roly-poly, and mash up six ounces of boiled potato with an ounce and a half of margarine, seasoning with pepper and perhaps a little salt. Mix in two heaped table-spoonfuls of grated cheese, and bind with two eggs. Whisk well together, and spread this mixture over the pastry. Roll up into a roly-poly, shape this into a crescent, brush it over with melted margarine or butter, and bake it in a greased baking-dish for half an hour in a moderate oven. A suitable sauce should be handed separately.

Potatoes and Cheese

Really old-fashioned, this. Boil some even-sized potatoes in their skins, and when they are done, peel them at once and pile them up in the middle of a dish. On serving, surround them with thin shavings of cheese sprinkled with cayenne pepper, and with a green salad on a separate plate.

Potatoes and Mushrooms

Chop up three or four spring onions, stew them for a little in a tablespoonful of butter or margarine, then add a pound and a half of peeled and sliced potatoes and cover and stew again for a quarter of an hour. Now mix in carefully a tablespoonful of flour, and moisten with half a pint of hot vegetable stock or milk or a mixture of both. Bring to the boil and add half a pound of peeled and sliced mushrooms, a tablespoonful of chopped parsley and a seasoning of salt and pepper. Put on the lid again, and simmer for another twenty minutes or so.

Potatoes and Onion

Peel some potatoes, slice them thinly and arrange them in overlapping layers in a greased fireproof dish, sprinkling each layer with salt, pepper and very finely minced onion. Just cover with milk, and bake in a slow oven until the top is browned and the potatoes done. Poached eggs served with this make a very good dish.

Potatoes and Tomatoes

Fry a finely chopped onion in a little butter or margarine until lightly browned, then add some roughly broken cooked potatoes, seasoning to taste with pepper and salt. Stir lightly together and add a breakfastcupful of mashed stewed tomatoes or tinned tomatoes and a little grated cheese. Cook together on a low heat, stirring gently now and again, for about ten minutes, and then serve at once. The potatoes should not be floury or in too small pieces, the aim being to see that they do not break up too much in the cooking. This could pleasantly be garnished with half-moons or triangles of pastry.

Potatoes Bretonne

Peel the potatoes and cut them in dice about one inch across. Chop up some onions, a trifle of garlic and a few skinned tomatoes, mix with the potato cubes, turn into a fireproof dish, just cover them with stock, and bake until the potatoes are done.

Potatoes Byron

Bake some potatoes in their jackets, and as soon as they are cooked, empty out the pulp and mash it up smoothly, adding salt and pepper and an ounce and a half of butter or margarine for each pound of the mashed potato- Spread this out as a thick cake in a frying-pan containing some very hot margarine or butter, and fry the cake brown on both sides. Now dish it in a fireproof dish, sprinkle it generously with grated cheese and cream, and brown it quickly in the oven or under the grill. Garnish with grilled tomatoes if you wish.

Potatoes Dauphinoise

There are two versions of this dish, but this is the one that I prefer, Rub a shallow fire- proof dish with a cut clove of garlic and then grease it well with butter or margarine. Peel and slice some raw potatoes thinly, and arrange them in layers in the dish, sprinkling each layer with salt, pepper and grated nutmeg. When the dish is nearly full, pour in a pint of milk into which you have well beaten an egg and two ounces of grated cheese. It should run down between the potato slices, which you will not have packed too tightly, and nearly cover them as well. Sprinkle the top with more grated cheese, and bake in a moderate oven for about an hour.

Potatoes en Casserole

Fry a chopped onion in a little butter or mar- garine, and put it into a casserole with two or three tomatoes, peeled and with the pips removed and cut small. Now add some thin slices of cold boiled potatoes, plenty of salt and pepper, a small piece of butter and a teacupful of stock. Stir all gently together, cover and cook in a moderate oven for about twenty minutes. Those who like garlic could fry a very little of it with the onion.

Potatoes Florentine

Cook some potatoes in their skins, and peel them while they are still hot. Spread a layer of spinach, rather dry, in the bottom of a greased shallow fireproof dish and arrange the sliced potatoes on this in an overlapping layer. Cover them with a rather thick cheese sauce, sprinkle the top with a little more grated cheese, and brown quickly.

Potatoes Grilled with Cheese

Cook some waxy potatoes in their skins, peel them while they are still hot, and cut them in slices about half an inch thick. Put these on a well-greased grid, sprinkle them with grated cheese (or a mixture of cheese and a few breadcrumbs), season with only a grain or two of cayenne pepper, and put them under the grill for the cheese to melt.

Potatoes in Onion Sauce

Cut some cooked potatoes into rings and arrange these, not too tightly, in a greased fire-proof dish. Now make a sauce like this. Chop up some spring onions and stew them in a little lard until they are soft. Add a little flour and enough water with a dash of vinegar to make a thinnish sauce, putting in a bay leaf and two or three cloves and seasoning with salt and pepper. Cook this gently for twenty minutes or so, then take out the bay leaf and cloves, and pour the sauce over the potatoes. They can be served hot as they are, or the top of the dish can be strewn with buttered breadcrumbs, and browned in the oven or under the grill.

Potatoes Niçoise

Bake some large floury potatoes in their jackets, and when they are done cut off a piece from the side of each, and scoop out a table-spoonful of the inside. Fill up these cavities with a mixture made of chopped and mashed fillets of anchovy, chopped parsley, minced garlic and black pepper moistened with some of the oil from the tin of anchovies. This must be made while the potatoes are baking, for they must be very hot when the mixture is put into them, so that the diners mash it at once into the pulp for their best enjoyment.

Potatoes Normande

Chop up the white part of one or two leeks and an onion as well, and fry them lightly in a little margarine or butter without browning them. Add some finely chopped raw potatoes, season with salt and pepper, put them into a fireproof dish and just cover them with milk, Bake in a moderate oven for about three-quarters of an hour, when the milk will have been absorbed into the vegetables and the top will be nicely browned.

Potatoes Provençale

Put some smoothly mashed potato in the bottom of a well-greased shallow fireproof dish, which you have first rubbed with a cut clove of garlic, and cover this with a good layer of thick tomato purée or even of stewed tomatoes provided that they are fairly dry. Sprinkle well with buttered crumbs mixed with chopped parsley, and brown the top quickly. Crisply fried eggs make a good garnish, but they must be cooked in very hot oil in a small saucepan, and not in the frying-pan in the more usual way, so that the white is gathered over the yolk and is golden and crisp outside.

Potatoes Vosgienne

Peel and cut some potatoes in thin slices, and arrange them in layers in a shallow fireproof dish which you have first rubbed with a cut clove of garlic and then greased with butter or margarine. Season each layer of potatoes lightly with salt and pepper, and when the dish is nearly full, cover the potatoes with cream, and cook them on a moderate heat. When the potatoes are tender, pour in a little more cream, put the dish under the grill or in a hot oven, and let the top get golden for serving.

Potatoes with Bread Sauce

Slice some parboiled potatoes, and grease a fireproof dish with butter or margarine. In the bottom of this put a thinnish layer of well-flavoured and smoothly made bread sauce, and upon this a layer of potatoes. Sprinkle with salt, pepper and nutmeg (unless there is nutmeg already in the sauce), and continue these layers until the dish is full. Let the last layer be of sauce, sprinkle this with browned breadcrumbs and bake for half an hour in a slowish oven. Garnish with baked or grilled tomato-halves.

Potatoes with Cheese

Cut some cooked potatoes into dice and put them into a greased fireproof dish. Make a thick cheese sauce, bind it with an egg-yolk, and pour it over the potato dice. Whisk the white stiffly, spread it on top of the sauce, sprinkle with a little more finely grated cheese, and brown in the oven.

Potatoes with Cheese
(Gratin Savoyard)

Chop up some raw potatoes very finely and season them with salt, pepper and grated nutmeg. Butter a shallow fireproof dish, put in a layer of the potatoes and cover it with grated Gruyère cheese. Then add more potatoes and more cheese, moisten with good stock, dot with butter, and cook on the top of the stove until the stock boils. Let it boil gently for ten minutes, then put the dish into a moderate oven, and bake until the top is golden and the stock has disappeared. Floury potatoes are best for this very famous dish.

Potatoes with Eggs

Boil half a dozen good-sized floury potatoes, mash them smoothly and beat them with an ounce of butter or margarine, three tablespoonfuls of warm milk, and a well-beaten egg. Put a layer of this purée into a buttered fireproof dish and on this arrange a layer of sliced hard-boiled egg. Sprinkle with salt and pepper, and continue the layers, ending with potato. Cover this with buttered crumbs, and bake in a hot oven until the top is nicely browned.

Potatoes with Mustard Sauce

Cook some potatoes in their skins, then peel them while they are hot and cut them into rather thick slices. Put these into a fireproof dish, and pour over them a sauce made by browning some flour in butter or margarine, thickening it with stock and seasoning it with salt, pepper and a good deal of French mustard. Cover the whole with breadcrumbs, sprinkle with melted butter or margarine, and brown lightly in the oven. The potato slices are sometimes first sauté before they are put into the dish.

Potatoes with Olives

Bake two pounds of potatoes in their jackets, peel them, mash them, and mix them with a quarter of a pint of warm milk, two ounces of grated cheese, preferably Gruyère, fifteen black olives, stoned and finely chopped, a seasoning of salt and pepper and the yolk of an egg. When mixed, add the stiffly-whisked egg-white. Turn the mixture into a well-greased soufflé dish which has been sprinkled with breadcrumbs, and bake it in a moderate oven for half an hour.

Stuffed Potatoes

There are a great number of varieties of these, and here are a few:

(1) Mix with the mashed pulp of baked potato half a dozen finely chopped anchovies, seasoning with a little grated nutmeg. Fill the skins with this mixture, sprinkle with grated cheese and a little melted butter or cream, and brown in the oven.

(2) Mix with the mashed pulp either two tablespoonfuls of grated cheese and the same of chopped tinned red sweet peppers, or two tablespoonfuls of chopped olives stuffed with red sweet pepper. (This is the usual filling for the stuffed olives normally sold in this country.) Pile the mixture lightly into the skins, and brown.

(3) Mix the mashed potato with egg-yolk, season it well, pile it up in the skins, and bake until the tops are browned, Chopped chives or parsley can be added to the mixture if desired.

(4) Add to the mashed pulp of half a dozen potatoes three coarsely sieved hard-boiled eggs and half a teacupful of grated cheese. Sprinkle the tops of the stuffed potatoes with more cheese, let it brown in the oven and finish with a pinch of paprika pepper.

Other simple suggestions are to mash the pulp with onion purée, alone or mixed with cheese or curry powder; with tomato purée, alone or mixed with cheese; with a third of its volume of cooked rice flavoured with grated cheese; with flaked smoked haddock, the stuffed skins being sprinkled afterwards with grated cheese and then browned.

Viennese Potatoes

Boil some waxy potatoes in their skins and peel them while still hot. Slice them and arrange them in a greased fireproof dish, seasoning with salt and pepper, and covering with a

layer of peeled and sliced tomatoes. Season
again, pour over a little cream and sprinkle well
with breadcrumbs. Then sprinkle these with
melted butter or margarine, and bake for half
an hour in a moderate oven, when the top
should be nicely browned. For a larger dish,
arrange the potatoes and tomatoes in alternate
layers, but always begin with potato and end
with tomato.

INDEX